Tumbleweed Tara

The Tumbly Road to Significance

Tumbleweed Tara

The Tumbly Road to Significance

Text copyright © 2009 by Shawne Barron

Illustrations copyright © 2009 by Steve Björkman

Published by True Potential Publishing, Inc.
PO Box 904 Travelers Rest, SC 29690
http://tppress.com

Tumbleweed Tara's *The Tumbly Road to Significance* and other True Potential Publishing books can be purchased at a discount by churches, ministries and other organizations for evangelical, educational or promotional use. For more information please write Special Markets Department, c/o True Potential Publishing, PO Box 904 Travelers Rest, SC 29690; or contact us via e-mail: info@tppress.com

Visit Tumbleweed Tara on the web at http://tumbleweedtara.com

First Printing 2009

ISBN: 978-0-9823059-4-2

LCCN: 2009920604

Printed in China

Thank You!

Thank you, Lord, for allowing me to be a part of Your project!

Thank you, Andy, my amazing husband, for being my A-number one best cheerleader, sponsor and "envisioner".

Thank you, Tim and Darcy, for being used so powerfully by God to supply that written-down inspiration for me and for folks everywhere.

Thank you, Steve and Elaine, that you've loved Tara such a heap to give her all these opportunities. (Can't wait, not even a bit, to tear into the ones to come...)

Endless thanks to Leah, for that wee-small time in your life when you chose to somersault hither and yon rather than walk, skip or sashay.

Shawne Barron

"Do nothing out of selfish ambition or vain conceit, but in humility consider others better than yourselves." (Philippians 2:3)

Ta daaaaaa! Mom's hands clapped!
Dad's whistle whistled!
"Hooray!" They cheered.
Tara turned a somersault!

Tara's kid sister Clara tried a somersault.

"Kinda inside-out and sideways, Clara. But watch me!" Tara hollered.

"Pretty perfect," Clara mumbled.

Tara went looking for a bigger audience.

"Bravo!" bellowed the barber.
"Beautiful somersault!"
"Incredible!" crowed the crowd.
Tara curtseyed. "Thank you, thank you."

At Tara's next show the crowd went hog-wild. "Five somersaults in a row! Wow!"

"More somersaults -- more clapping and cheering for me!" thought Tara

"I've got to practice! I'm somebody special.
Boy, am I ...
am I ... ohhh ... what's the word?"
"You're significant!" chimed in Clara.
"That's it! I'm significant!"

Five, six, seven somersaults in a row --
eight, nine, ten,
and Tara was still going --
eleven, twelve.

All of the sudden, a swift wind
blew down and gave her a
giant boost.
Wheeeee! Boy hidee, was she
rolling now!

Leaves stuck to her hair and
socks.

They itched and itched, but
scratch, she could not, --
she was rolling too fast.

Clunk! Tara tumbled over
Mr. Clem's junk pile.

A stinky rubber boot was now
stuck in her somersault!
Pee-yuuuuu!

Splink, snap!
What now?
Miss Snodgrass's
pink flamingos!!

Mee-ooww!!
Whose MEOW was that?

Tara tumbled and tumbled.
She was somersaulting down
open road, faster than a
greased pig.
"Help!" she shouted as she
passed the telephone man.
"I can't stop!"

"Well hush my mouth! That's the first talking tumbleweed I've ever seen," marveled the telephone man. He chased after the tumbleweed.

A big crowd followed behind.
They had never seen a talking tumbleweed
before!

Zoooooom went the telephone truck.
"We'll save you!" shouted the crowd.
"I sure hope so," cried the tumbleweed.

Faster and faster tumbled the tumbleweed.
Faster and faster raced the truck.

Arms stretched and hands reached, BUT no one could get that tumbleweed!

"I'll never stop spinning!" exclaimed the dizzy tumbleweed.

In a shot, little Clara swung out her umbrella which hooked the tumbleweed right nicely, indeed.

"Hooray!" hollered the crowd.
"At last!" sighed the tumbleweed.

"What now?" asked the telephone man.
"Untangle me!" shouted the tumbleweed.

"My cat!" declared Mrs. Meek.
"My flamingos!" sneered Miss Snodgrass.
"My boot?" wondered Mr. Clem.
"My Tara!" cried Tara's mom.

"Well done, Clara!" shouted the Mayor.
Clara curtsied a delicate 'thank you'.
"Incredible!" crowed the crowd.

"TRULY INCREDIBLE!!" cheered Tara.
They all clapped for Clara.

"Mom and Dad, it sure 'nuf makes me feel all warm down deep inside when I clap for Clara," said Tara.

"Well Miss Tumbleweed Tara," her mom replied, "that's because you are somebody real special. Why, you're downright significant, and Clara is too -- because God loves you both so much, and so do your mom and dad!"

""Hoo-wee! We're significant --
just the way we are!"
Tara and Clara agreed.

A Note to Parents from Dr. Kimmel:

What can we learn from Tara?

All children are born with three driving inner needs. They need to know that they are *secure*, they're *significant*, and they're *strong*. The best way to meet these needs is by consistently giving your children a *secure* love, a *significant* purpose in life, and a *strong* hope for the future.

Tumbleweed Tara longed to feel significant. So did her little sister Clara. Tara thought that significance was based on something that she could do better than someone else – like somersaults. But she found out quickly that a one-dimensional ability is not enough to satisfy that need. Clara wasn't as talented as her older sister – at least when it came to doing somersaults, yet she saved Tara when her somersaulting got out of control. Both were good at something, but their wise parents reminded them that their true significance wasn't just found in what they could do, but more in the fact that they were deeply loved by their parents and by God, regardless of how well they performed their respective talents.

Kids can gain a great deal of significance by perfecting their God-given talents. But they need to know that despite their talent, their primary significance comes from the sheer fact that they are … that they exist as human beings and that they are dearly loved by the God who made them and the parents who raise them.

Discussion questions for your child:

1. Tara was great at doing somersaults. Have you ever wanted to be the best at something?

2. How do you think Clara felt when she couldn't do somersaults as well as Tara? Have you ever felt that way about someone else?

3. When Clara was able to help Tara stop the tumbling out of control, how could that change the way they viewed each other? How could it change the way they viewed themselves?

4. What did their parents teach Tara and Clara about their real value?

Dr. Tim Kimmel is the Executive Director of Family Matters® whose goal is to equip parents to raise truly great kids through the power of God's grace. Grace-based parenting is a comprehensive strategy for parenting that shows moms and dads how to treat their children the same way God treats His – with grace. It's a powerful plan for raising kids that shows parents how to maintain a loving balance between rules and relationship, automatically bring the best out of everyone in the family portrait, and intrinsically draw your child's heart to the heart of God.

The grace-based strategy for raising kids has four basic components:

- Creating an atmosphere of grace in your home
- Meeting your child's three true inner needs
- Building your child's character
- Aiming your child at a future of true greatness

Tim conducts parenting conferences throughout the U.S. and Canada. His books, _Grace Based Parenting_, _Raising Kids Who Turn Out Right_ and _Raising Kids for True Greatness_ develop in depth the grace-based strategy. For more information on grace based parenting and to learn more about the books and DVD's by Tim Kimmel, just go to _www.familymatters.net_.

Tim and his wife Darcy have raised four children and have a growing number of grandchildren.

Tara's creator, Shawne Barron, just happens to habitate right smack dab in the middle of Texas with her fun-loving husband, three sons and two daughters, four donkeys, one cat, one dog ... not to mention the patch of fairly decent watermelons. She is a wife, mom, research author and pediatric dentist who has yet to tumble anywhere near as fast as her own tumbleweeds.

Tara's illustrator, Steve Björkman, has been drawing professionally for thirty years and has illustrated more than eighty children's books and countless greeting cards. Steve and his wife live in California, along with their three children, a cat, a dog, and a desert tortoise, who, coincidently, is very fond of watermelons."

For more Tumbleweed Tara adventures visit: http://tumbleweedtara.com